Maggie Roberts

Shadows and Silver Sprays

Maggie Roberts

Shadows and Silver Sprays

ISBN/EAN: 9783743323308

Manufactured in Europe, USA, Canada, Australia, Japa

Cover: Foto ©ninafisch / pixelio.de

Manufactured and distributed by brebook publishing software (www.brebook.com)

Maggie Roberts

Shadows and Silver Sprays

BY
EIGGAM STREBO

NEW YORK:
JOHN F. TROW & SON.
1875.

DEDICATION.

THIS book is respectfully dedicated to the National Guard of New York, who, "Heroically, Physically, and Mentally," cannot be excelled by any troops in the world. Each poem is to the point; therefore it is needless for the author to say more than that they command the admiration and respect of their own, and every other nation.

	PAGE
THE NATION'S GUARD OF HONOR	1
UNITED WE STAND	3
TO THE NATIONAL GUARD	5
THE BRAVE BOYS IN BLUE	7
'TWAS BUT A DREAM	8
THE TWO GREAT OAKS	11
TO THE GALLANT NINTH REGIMENT	13
FAITH	15
BOYS, THAT FLAG MUST FALL	16
THE DEAD WARRIOR PRESIDENT	18
LINES UPON THE ABSENCE OF MY HUSBAND	20
STAY WITH ME, SISTER, IF ONLY IN SLEEP	21
DEATH OF THE CHRISTIAN HERO	23
OUT IN THE STORM	25
TO A LOVER UPON HIS MISTRESS	27
SONG OF WELCOME TO ALEXIS	29
ALEXIS CELEBRATING THE BIRTHDAY OF HIS SISTER-IN-LAW	30
ACROSTIC ON THE "GRAND DUKE ALEXIS"	32
ALEXIS CONTEMPLATING THE RUINS OF CHICAGO	33
A NATIONAL ACROSTIC—RUSSIA AND AMERICA	37

CONTENTS.

	PAGE
THE TWO ALEXANDERS	39
BORN IN A MANGER	41
CHRISTMAS MORN	42
THE DYING YEAR	44
FAREWELL TO 1871	45
HAPPY NEW-YEAR	49
ALEXIS OUT ON THE PLAINS	50
FLOUNDERING IN THE RAIN	52
TWILIGHT MUSING	54
SLEIGHING BY MOONLIGHT	55
"KIND WORDS WILL NEVER DIE"	57
I WILL BE THINE	58
OUR STARS AND BARS	59
MOSES RECEIVING THE TEN COMMANDMENTS	61
MOONLIGHT	62
THE YOUNG SOUTHERN HUNTERS	63
THE EXPLOSION OF THE WESTFIELD	64
CONSOLATION	66
EASTER MORN	67
GRATITUDE	68
SHALL AMERICANS RULE AMERICA?	71
DEATH OF THE YOUNG DRAGOON	73
DEATH	75
IS MY SISTER DEAD?	76
THE SILVER STREAM IN A SOLID ROCK	78
THE ASSASSINATION OF THE PRINCE OF ERIE	80
O GOD! TAKE THOU HIS SOUL	82
LOVE	83

CONTENTS.

	PAGE
THE LAST WORDS OF A DYING YOUNG CHRISTIAN	84
A VISION DURING ILLNESS	86
ON THE DEATH OF AN INFANT	88
TO MY FOSTER-BROTHER	89
LIFE'S SILVER THREAD IS BROKEN	90
LINES ON THE DEATH OF MARY R——, OF WASHINGTON CITY	92
THE WRECK OF THE PASINO	94
AN ACROSTIC—CONFIDENCE	97
THE SERENADE	98
WALKING DOWN BROADWAY	99
SEA OF MATRIMONY	100
TO A BACHELOR	101
FLIRTATION	101
TAMMANY RING	102
THE GHOST OF PATTERLOO	104
THE RIVAL SPIRITS	106
ANGELS' SONG	107
VILLAGERS' BURIAL SONG	107
FAIRYS' SONG	108
CHILDREN'S BOAT SONG	109
INCANTATION SONG	110
WITCHES' SONG	111
ODE TO THE MOON	112
SONG IN THE DISTANCE	112
ESTRALDA'S SONG	113
ANSWER BY APOLLYON	113

The last Songs—from the Original Plays—by the Author.

CONTENTS.

	PAGE
THE KING'S PETITION	114
ANSWER BY ESTRALDA	114
CHORAL SONG	116
THE AUTHOR'S APPEAL AND ADIEU	117

THE NATION'S GUARD OF HONOR.

ALL hail! to the gallant sons of Mars
In time of peace, in time of wars,
To their honor be it henceforth said,
They're worth something more than a dress parade.

In a moment when danger threatens our land,
Round our loved banner undaunted they stand;
And with pride the flag of the free is unfurled,
As an harbinger of love and peace to the world.

To all nations an hearty welcome we give,
With this as our motto, "We live, and let live;"
But beware how ye tamper with the laws of our nation,
For the avenger is nigh ye, no matter your station.

Our flag was bought with a nation's best blood,
And for ninety-five years in pride it has stood
Firmly planted on land—and it floats o'er the sea
To let all the world know that America is free.

'Tis the flag of the free that our forefathers gave,
To prove that their sons will ne'er cringe like a slave;
For under its folds ye must conquer or die,
With victory or death "as your last battle cry."

UNITED WE STAND.

Hip! hip! hurrah! boys,
Fill up, fill up the wine;
Let us drink this day
To the boys in gray
From over Mason and Dixon's line.

Hip! hip! hurrah! boys,
Fill up, fill up the bowl;
For as brothers we stand
In defence of our land
Whenever her honor calls roll.

Hip! hip! hurrah! boys,
As we grasp each guardsman's hand,
Let this be our toast,
"We welcome the boast,
And pride of old Maryland."

Hip! hip! hurrah! boys,
Let the welkin ring this day,
 As with *three times three*,
 And a tiger, you see,
We welcome the boys in gray.

TO THE NATIONAL GUARD.

They care no more for Orangemen
   Than any other cause;
But they do love their country,
   And will maintain her laws;
So at the first tap of the drum
Thousands to guard her honor come.

Nobly they bear their heritage,
   The banner of the free;
And come with an undaunted front,
   That all the world may see
That they are willing to die,
For their free and glorious country.

Then to our noble guardsmen,
   Who on that fearful day
Lay wounded on the pavement
   In the sun's hot, scorching ray,

We give our gratitude to you,
Ye gallant braves, all tried and true.

Well done, ye good and faithful,
　Ye've well earned your reward;
And justice shall be meted out
　To the brave "National Guard,"
Who responsive to their teachings came
To vindicate fair Freedom's name.

And for your noble sacrifice,
　Of Wyatt, Prior, and Page,
Their memory 'll live in every heart
　Of this and, the coming age;
And tears will flow when ye shall tell
How nobly those three guardsmen fell.

THE BRAVE BOYS IN BLUE.

CHEERFULLY to the rescue came
　　The gallant men in blue;
Protestant and Catholic the same,
　　We tender thanks to you
For espousing first our country's cause,
To punish those who break her laws.

Death's missiles flew so thick and fast
　　Around those men in blue;
They heeded not the raging blast,
　　For they were tried and true,—
Stern guardians of our nation's laws,
Willing to die in Freedom's cause.

Onward they come; a solid front
　　Present those men in blue;
Ready to bear the battle's brunt,
　　And to die for me and you.
Then let us give our heartfelt thanks
To the handsome, bold, police phalanx.

"'TWAS BUT A DREAM."

I DREAMED a dream;
Yet was it all a dream?
Methought I stood upon a rock,
Far above the level of the sea,
Whose angry waves lashed in their fury,
As they vied with each other in their fierce attack
Upon the gallant vessels that were homeward
      bound,
And made their sturdy timbers groan in agony.
              But while I seemed to be
Transfixed with horror to the spot,
A rushing sound hard by aroused me:
So I just turned in time to 'scape great danger.
Methought I turned my gaze upon the land,
And there behold'st—what!
A train of cars upon an awful precipice,
Ready to topple o'er.
The rushing sound that I had heard before
Was caused by two small boats

Cutting through the sand to rescue them
From their impending doom.
Ere I had time, as 'twere, to wake from wonder,
A huge vessel did speed past me,
And dashed itself o'er the great precipice
Into the seething waves below. A sound
As if an earthquake shook the ground—
A shroud of darkness wrapped itself o'er all—
The angry waves roared terribly,
But could not wholly engulf this thing
Which lay embedded there
Quivering like some great giant
In death's last throes.
     Again methought,
As I in sorrow turned away,
A stranger faced me, and thus spake he:
Friend! dost thou not comprehend?
List ye, while I enlighten thee.
This nation shall be shortly shaken
By some one's sudden taking off,
But his good deeds shall not forgotten be.
See'st thou his quivering form,
Yon waves dare not cover;

Mark ye my words—" Farewell!"
And as he spoke, the stranger vanished,
And I was left in darkness:
I could see and hear no more.

"THE TWO GREAT OAKS."

Woman! behold thy work,
Two sturdy oaks blasted by the lightning
Of thy foul, licentious love.
The great oak under whose sheltering branches
Thou hast basked in the sunshine of prosperity
Has fallen;
And by its fall society is shaken
E'en to its very centre;
And thy base ingratitude laid bare
Before an indignant world.

The lesser oak, around which twined
A tender clinging vine,
Which only did one little blossom bear,
Now lies rent and blackened
By thy foul lightning stroke.
How shall this vine its loss sustain?
Shall it lose its hold upon this blackened trunk,
And fold its tiny blossom to its breast and die?

Or shall it cling more closely to its former love,
And hurl down curses on thy head,
Which justly is thy portion?

Bold plotter and base ingrate,
We leave thee to thy conscience,
Which surely must consume thee
With the fires of Hell. [*See remark.*]

TO THE GALLANT NINTH REGIMENT.

And tears will flow when ye shall tell
How nobly those three guardsmen fell.

TO THE GALLANT NINTH REGIMENT.

Ay! glory to the Ninth, ye firm, tried, and true,
A great people tender sincere thanks to you;
And their tears of sympathy shall freely flow
For your brave young comrades thus laid low.

From the ruffian's hand the fatal bullet sped,
And they were numbered along with the dead;
So with solemn tread and the muffled drum,
Ye have laid three heroes away in the tomb.

And when the pages of history shall tell,
In defending Columbia's fair fame how they fell,
Covered with glory, yet their blood ye shall see
Has nurtured the tree of our sweet liberty.

Ah! where is your chief, that led in the fray,
With no semblance of rank, on that fatal day?
He fell in the charge, struggling with might,
To maintain law and order, justice and right.

TO THE GALLANT NINTH REGIMENT.

Bowed down with grief is this great lion-hearted,
And affection's tears flow for the heroes departed;
They have fought their last fight, the victory is
    won,
And the Angels have whispered, Brothers, come
    home.   *[See remark.]*

"FAITH."

The waves of time may madly lash
   Around my stronghold of defence;
Down at its base there comes no crash,
   Armed is my fortress, in one sense.
So in many years of coming time
   Retreating waves will murmur low;
And thro' life's mist a star shall shine
   To guide me where pure waters flow.

Waters of pleasure, in whose bright spray
   I hope to make my bark secure;
So when the Master calls—I may
   Rest me well when life is o'er.
I have built my faith upon that Rock
   Of Ages, which shall always be,
Ere fleeting memory shall me mock.
   Oh! lasting Rock, I cling to thee.

BOYS, THAT FLAG MUST FALL!

See yonder flag float in the breeze,
    I wonder why it waves at all;
Hear me, brave boys, for by my faith
    I swear to you that flag must fall.

No sooner were the rash words spoken,
    Than he left behind his comrades all,
Rushed madly on in his blind fury,
    Shouting aloud, that flag shall fall.

Instead of calling his men around him,
    Gallantly to scale the outer wall,
And tear away the rebel emblem,
    That seemed obnoxious to them all;

He went alone, with sword uplifted,
    Shouting, as he rushed through the hall,
I'll strike to death all who oppose me,
    For I have sworn that flag shall fall.

Onward he rushed, the stairs ascending
  The roof once gained, flag, staff, and all
Was in his grasp, while he with boasting,
  Cried, Said I not this flag should fall?

What gained he by his reckless daring?
  Nought but death from pistol-ball,
Shot through the heart while he was coming
  Down the stairs of Marshall Hall.

THE DEAD WARRIOR PRESIDENT.

STAND back amazed, in reverence hold thy breath,
This man, whom armies lately did command,
  Now silent lies in death.
Bend low thy head, let fall the silent tear
When thou around the illustrious dead shall stand,
  And breathe a solemn prayer.

Short was his race as statesman great, he run;
He was more fitted for the tented field
  Than in palatial home—
Foremost was always found in thickest of the fray;
Like warrior of old, his trusty sword would wield,
  His country's foe to slay.

This hero heeds no more the early bugle call,
But lays at rest, with arms cross't o'er his breast,
    Upon his funeral pall.
He'll stand no more amid loud cannons' rattle;
His work is done, the warrior takes his rest
    From life's last battle.

LINES UPON THE ABSENCE OF MY HUSBAND.

At silent eve I miss thee most,
When night draws out her shining host;
No kindred spirit near me lies,
To watch the wonders of the skies.

No husband's arm around me thrown,
Nor manly breast to lean upon,
But ever thinking of the bliss
Of love's last thrilling, lingering bliss.

Oh, would I were a bird, I'd fly,
Imprisoned in thine arms to lie;
And love's impassioned words to hear
From lips that are to me so dear.

Tho' stern fate th' material part,
Yet soul to soul and heart to heart
Cries out in ecstasy—oh, bliss!
Earth ne'er can claim more love than this.

STAY WITH ME, SISTER, IF ONLY IN SLEEP.

CANST thou come back to me from the echoless shore,
And reign in my heart as in days of yore,
Let my kisses once more press thy damask cheek,
And in my strong arms be rocked gently to sleep?

Ah! only in dreams wilt thou come back to me,
In the land of shadows I can mingle with thee;
But waking, there's no loved one to welcome me home;
I must roam through the wide world sad and alone.

Come, then, in my dreams, and drive away care,
Let thy soft loving touch fall on my dark hair,
Over thy brother a tender watch keep—
Stay with me, sister, if only in sleep.

STAY WITH ME, SISTER, IF ONLY IN SLEEP.

Let me clasp thee once more in a loving embrace,
With thy light silken lashes just sweeping my face;
Oh! come to me sister, if only in sleep,
And over thy brother a loving watch keep.

DEATH OF THE CHRISTIAN HERO.

A PALL of deep gloom is spread o'er our land,
For the mighty has fallen, but not by man's hand,
'Twas the voice of his Maker that called him away,
And a great people mourn for the hero to-day.
Toll, toll ye your bells for the chieftain departed,
Let affection's tears flow for the great lion-hearted.

Who, who, since the days of our great Washington,
Is mourned so sincere as Virginia's proud son?

With the Christian's pure faith all trials he o'ercame,
And the world will henceforth revere his great name.
With artillery's dull roar, and the roll of the drum,
Ye must lay the great hero away in the tomb.

OUT IN THE STORM.

'Twas on a gloomy winter's day,
    Sad and alone I wandered on;
No hand outstretched to lead the way,
    Or shield me from the pelting storm.

While scalding tears coursed down my cheek,
    Messengers from an o'ercharged heart;
Lethiferous gloom I fain would seek,
    Nor with the world would grieve to part.

Loud roared the blast, fierce was the gale,
    I bowed before its dread attack—
And heard as 'twere a human wail
    From out its depths cry, Hold! come back!

Some unseen power impelled me on,
    Strength was girded about me then—
I followed blindly a phantom form,
    And soon forgot "what might have been."

Before me a regal being stood,
   And welcomed me with gentle voice;
So glorious in true womanhood
   It made my sinking heart rejoice.

Not with vain words did she beguile
   A sister in distress like me,
But with substantial gifts the while,
   Made me feel happy, light, and free.

Her beauty rare and queenly mien,
   Must cause her to act well her part;
But *I* her better self have seen—
   I know her great unselfish heart.

May she accept my grateful song,
   'Tis all that I in turn can give
For all the kindness done to one
   In whose memory she will ever live.

And when her work on earth is done,
   Let deeds like these remembered be;
So, angels bright shall guide her home
   To the mansions of eternity.

TO A LOVER UPON HIS MISTRESS.

AMAZED thou may be
When thou shalt trace
The living truth that I vouchsafe
Upon this quiet page;
Forsooth I will straight to the purpose come,
Or else thou'lt think the writer's wit outrun.

Know, then, thou hold'st a jewel rare,
Enshrined in a casket of such perfect workman-
    ship
That methinks 'twould need none other
Than a homely front
To shed its brilliancy around,
And cause thy pulses with delight to bound.

I'll solve the problem here at once,
'Tis of thy queenly love that I would speak;
The jewel is the great unselfish heart

That its pure sympathy can give;
No empty boasting form the sweet lips flow,
But cheering words to alleviate another's woe.

The lovely setting of this rare jewel,
May be admired, nay be courted,
By a sycophantic world;
But only those with daily intercourse
Must know its priceless worth:
Guard well the treasure that your God has given
To light your life this side of heaven.

SONG OF WELCOME TO ALEXIS.

WE hail thee! Alexis,
   Bold son of the sea;
And bid thee most welcome
   To the land of the free,
We'll say to thee, gallant tar,
   As thro' our land ye roam,
Welcome, Alexis,
   Pray feel at home.

We hail thee! Imperial Prince,
   Son of Russia's great Czar;
Beneficent in time of peace,
   Most terrible in war;
We'll shout an hearty welcome
   Wheresoe'er thou shalt roam,
Noble Alexis,
   Pray feel at home.

ALEXIS CELEBRATING THE BIRTHDAY OF HIS SISTER-IN-LAW.

What though in Columbia's free land thou dost roam,
Let thy thoughts ever turn towards kindred and home;
To thy parents, who deem thee the pride of their life,
And the lovely young " Czarovna," thy brother's young wife,
Whose health thou must drink in a far distant land,
With the hearty good wishes, of our true loyal band.

When in the Lord's temple thy prayers thou shalt say,
Asking many returns of this auspicious day;

For thy loving sister, far o'er the deep sea
Who is offering up prayers for the welfare of
 thee :
Oh! when the time comes to act her royal part
May she sway with affection the great Russian
 heart.

ACROSTIC ON THE "GRAND DUKE ALEXIS."

Great art thou in nature's treasures,
   Ranking high with sons of earth;
And amid thy royal pleasures,
   Nought can quell thy generous mirth.
Dear art thou to sister—brother,
   Doubly thou, to parents dear;
Under whose kind royal guidance,
   Know'st thou (with perception clear)
Entering into manhood sphere.

And amid thy royal wanderings,
   Let the first thoughts of thine heart
Enter freely thine home circle,
   Xylo-graph them each in part.
In thy collection let them lie,
   Show only, when thou, homeward hie.

ALEXIS CONTEMPLATING THE RUINS OF CHICAGO.

WHAT came I out to see?
A city in whose heart
The sword of flame didst pierce.
Ah, ruthless spirit!
Why didst thou pierce the heart
Of this great and beauteous Queen,
The young bride of the stalwart West,
Ere she did celebrate her golden wedding?
Thy foul tongue didst lick 'round her throne
And undermine its firm foundation
So it soon toppled o'er.
Then didst thou laugh in mockery
At her misery;
And with thy fiery fiends
Didst leap upon her court,
And with relentless fury
Wrench the sceptre from her hand

And lay her in the dust.
Oh, thou foul demon,
Monster thou, insatiate,
To wrap this beauteous Queen in flames
And hurl her down
Into the abyss of woe.
But she is not forever lost;
For in a little while this great Chicago will,
Phœnix like, rise from her ashes
And startle the world into admiration.
Ah! a sympathetic world sends forth
Pure messengers from its heart,
To lull the pain of her great desolation,
And bid her royal spouse hope on;
That ere many moons shall wane
He will clasp his resuscitated bride
To his broad bosom;
And not only celebrate their golden wedding,
But the centurial birth
Of this great Republic.
                              Enterprise
Hath set its seal upon this suffering court:
For while the hot breath of the expiring mon-
    ster

Still lingers mid its desolation,
Young walls begin to grow apace,
Under the touch of willing hands
And stout hearts.
Let me predict (from observation)
That soon temples of splendor
And massive arches
Will rise as if by magic o'er her ruins
And obliterate all traces
Of this fiery scourge.

Were I ever to forget
The hearty words of welcome
That on every side did me beset
When my foot first press't
This desolated court
Indeed I would an ingrate be;
       For surely!
The reverence in which this people
Hold my Imperial Sire,
Makes my young blood bound in my veins
With joy and gratitude to those
Who hail me as a brother.

Oh! may this link of friendship never severed
    be;
And I, when at my father's court
Recount the grandeur of this great Republic,
Will not fail to mention thee,
O, once fair and beauteous Queen,
The now desolate, but not disconsolate
Bride of the young West.
             Farewell!
But not forever.
Yet a little while I leave thee;
But will come again
To celebrate with thee
Thy century birth.
Again, Oh, Queen, farewell.
Though lost to sight,
I hold thee to my heart, Forever.

A NATIONAL ACROSTIC.

RUSSIA.

RANK'ST thou among earth's highest courts,
Upon escutcheons thine, no blot is found
Sullying thy fair fame.
So like thy Sister o'er the sea,
In setting all thy bondsmen free,
Art winning an eternal name.

AND.

Ah! what shall break fair friendship's chain,
Neatly and strong each link is formed
Drawing two great nations into one.

AMERICA.

Amongst us came a young stranger fair,
'Mid shouts prolonged, and clarion clear,
Echo rolled back like waves of the sea.
Russia's welcome to the land of the free.

A NATIONAL ACROSTIC.

In future may the "Eagle and the great Bear,"
Count the links in the chain of friendship they
   wear,
America and Russia, as one shall appear.

EMPEROR OF RUSSIA LIBERATING THE SERFS.

Henceforth as freemen ye go forth
To mix with nations of the earth.

THE TWO ALEXANDERS.

Thy prototype, O Russian Czar,
Was great, but thou art greater far,
For did'st thou not redemption bring
To millions who felt serfdom's sting?
Know'st thou all earth thy name shall bless,
For saving them from dire distress.
The knout thou hast put out of sight,
Which nought but terror and affright
Could make poor wretches such as they
Their hard task-master's will obey.
Thy kindly hand their shackles break,
And all their vengeful passions slake,
For while in bondage they would brood
O'er their foul wrong in wrathful mood.
But now from serfdom they come forth,
To mix with freemen of the earth:
And while in other lands they rove,
They tell of thy most wondrous love

In raising up their prostrate forms,
And righting all their grievous wrongs.

Oh, gracious Monarch! mighty Czar;
Thou art the greater, yet by far;
Than he who sat him down and wept
Because no more his conquering step
Could force the nations to obey
His foul and rank imperial sway;
To lift his sword in blood and strife,
Was the great feature of his life.
But thou, in thy triumphant car,
Wants nought to do with horrid war.
For thou a greater deed hath done
Than he who bloody victories won.
Millions of freemen own thy sway,
And all thy great commands obey.
So when thy journey here is o'er,
Thy praise shall sound from shore to shore.

BORN IN A MANGER.

While shepherds their flocks were watching,
The wise men from Eastward were marching,
Led on by a bright morning star,

Which stopped as they reached a lone manger,
As much as to say here's the stranger,
Whom to worship ye've come from afar.

In amazement themselves questioned mild,
And wondered what manner of child
In a stable like this should be born.

When an angel appeared, just in time
To proclaim He's of David's great line
Fear not but hail this glad morn.

CHRISTMAS MORN.

All hail this glad morn!
    The best day of the year;
For, through the wide world,
    It bringeth good cheer.
Peace, and good will on earth,
    Unto us is now given,
And angels shout loud
    Hallelujahs in Heaven.

'Tis the birth-day of Christ,
    Our dear brother and friend,
On whom all our bright hopes
    Of salvation depend.
We'll shout the glad tidings,
    Loud praise shall be given,
While the echo rolls through
    The great arches of heaven.

CHRISTMAS MORN.

Oh! who could be sad
    Upon this auspicious morn?
When this great prince of peace,
    Our Saviour, was born.
'Tis true, in a manger,
    With beast of the stall,
But we hail him "Our Monarch,"
    "Our Saviour," and all.

THE DYING YEAR.

Thy sands of life are nearly run,
And twelve month's labors almost done;
Fire, flood, and strife, has marked thy way,
O'er nature thou hast held full sway.

But thou art only sent from God
To make earth feel his chastening rod;
Then die, old year, without one pang,
We would not have thee back again.

'Tis solemn tho'! at midnight hour,
Thou'lt yield the sceptre of thy power
To the young hands of seventy-two,
Who may deal more cruel e'en than you.

Thousands will watch thy dying throes,
And gently will thy eye-lids close;
Bid thee farewell, while bells shall toll,
And death's dark waters o'er thee roll.

FAREWELL TO 1871.

WRAPPED in his winding sheet the old king lay,
Three days before his taking off,
As if loath to yield his breath
Ere the birth of his lusty heir.
Young eighteen hundred and seventy-two.
              (Oh, who can tell
What his career may be)
During the twelve months' reign
Of this expiring monarch,
Famine, sickness, and terrible disaster,
Held high revel at his court.
And millions are eager this day
To sing a requiem
Ere the solemn midnight tolling of the bells
Tells of his departure.
            Yet old seventy-one is not to blame.
Some of his predecessors have been
As relentless as himself.
Now let us look upon the bright side

Of this expiring year.
Has he not brought joy and gladness
To many an household?
Does not the miser's heart leap with joy
And his eyes scintillate
When counting o'er his treasure
Which this now expiring year has brought him.
   Then again;
Has he not filled earth's granaries,
And made fair fields nod pleasantly
In the bright sunshine and glistening summer
  showers?
Nature herself could not breathe without time,
Who, when his course is run
Must, like the sun, sink quietly to rest.
   Yet unlike the god of day,
Who rises from his slumbers to greet Aurora;
He goes hence, to be no more seen.

With what joy we hail the glad New Year;
Ah! had we the prescience of his career,
We might not be so demonstrative in our joy.
Yet enthusiastic nature

Always welcomes something new.
But now farewell, old year!
Nature herself seems weeping
O'er thine impending doom,
Which none can avert,
For the decree has gone forth
That thou shalt die.
We will e'en go down to the brink
Of the dark river with thee;
But none can draw thy feet
From the turbulent billows that surge round them,
And will so soon engulf thee forever.

We too must die, old seventy-one,
But not as thou die'st,
For we will rise again,
Having put on blessed immortality.
But thou! Ah, thou shall never rise again
Thou art dead—dead
For all eternity.
Again, old year, farewell!
Whate'er the faults of thy short reign hath been.

They shall be buried with thee.
                Oh, cruel king,
Roll up thy scroll—
Yield up thy sceptre—
And depart in peace.
                And
While on bended knee at solemn midnight hour,
When bells shall toll thy coming dissolution,
We will make a new covenant
With Him who upholds the universe,
And bids time roll on.
Though at the end of every twelvemonth
Each who is subservient to the Omnific,
Renders up his accounts
And rests from his labors,
For evermore.

HAPPY NEW YEAR.

With joyful salutations
  We hail the glad New Year,
And unto all earth's nations
  We hope t'will bring good cheer.
But what for us—
  Hast thou in view,
Oh, bright, young year,
  Of seventy-two.

While merry-merry bells
  Peal forth throughout the earth;
To watching, wondering millions tells
  The history of thy birth.
Now, what for us
  Hast thou in view,
Oh, bright New Year
  Of seventy-two.

ALEXIS OUT ON THE PLAINS.

Oh! naughty Custer, fie for shame,
That you should kiss this dusky dame
    In presence of his highness;
Who should have had, precedence sure,
For most effectually 'twould cure
    This maiden of her shyness.

To be kissed by this "hunter bold,"
And list to his stories ofttimes told,
    Of bear hunts "with his father;"
When he would take right royal aim,
And in fine style bring down his game,
    Leave it for serfs to gather.

You say pshaw! she don't comprehend:
Nought but what gifts the Duke would send,
    But that she understands you.
So she spreads her blanket on the floor,
And into it all good things pour:
    Off trots this charming Sioux.

Now, naughty Custer, won't you miss,
This maid from whom you snatched a kiss,
    Mid all assembled there—
Know you full well how she will rave
About the handsome, gallant brave,
    With flowing yellow hair.

FLOUNDERING IN THE RAIN.

There goes my umbrella,
   Turned inside out again;
Bless me, this is pleasant,
   Walking in the rain.

Jostled up together,
   I wonder if we're sane?
To think that this is pleasant,
   Walking in the rain.

With skirts tucked up a little,
   And boots about high tide,
We take the chances of a walk,
   And also of a slide.

Laughing at everybody
   As we go bobbing 'round,
And think it awful "jolly,"
   Sliding o'er the ground.

FLOUNDERING IN THE RAIN.

Picking up each other,
  We try it o'er again;
Here we go, and there we go—
  Splashing in the rain.

But where's my umbrella?
  Its gone and turned again;
Oh; is this not delightful,
  Walking in the rain.

Ah! when we turn the corner,
  'Twill all come right again;
For then we'll just be facing
  This splashing, dashing rain.

We'll soon forget our troubles,
  As we reach home again;
Oh, bless me, this is pleasant,
  Floundering in the rain.

TWILIGHT MUSING.

The shades of night are falling fast
   As thoughts are straying o'er the past;
Busy with scenes of joy and gloom
   But hark! there's voices in the room.

Methinks I hear the angels say,
   Come sister spirit soar away;
Enter through the portals bright
   The city of eternal light.

Leave all the cares of earth behind,
   At peace must be with all mankind;
Join our bright and happy throng
   Sing with us our heavenly song.

SLEIGHING BY MOONLIGHT.

Tinkle—tinkle,
   Hear the sleigh-bells jingle;
As we glide o'er the hard crusted snow
   And with shouts of laughter!
We race still faster,
   While old Boreas deals a sharp blow.

Although it is night,
   Yet the glorious light—
Of the moon shed its lustre around;
   For in its bright ray,
It appears as noonday
   And in safety we skim o'er the ground

So with the merry jingle,
   Gay laughter doth mingle;
While the crack of the whip gives great tone,
   And the fiery steeds do snort;
As the gay quick retort
   Goes round as we turn towards home.

Oh, we never can forget,
  That handsome naughty set
Of young gallants that followed in our train;
  We were never left alone,
In sunshine and in storm
  And fast friends we shall ever more remain.

"KIND WORDS WILL NEVER DIE."

I was a very little boy,
   Not more than two foot high;
When I first ever learned to sing,
   "Kind words, will never die."

I would sing it to the soldiers,
   And ofttimes make them cry;
When they would say, what made you sing
   "Kind words will never die."

I said because you left your homes,
   And all that you hold dear;
To camp among us strangers
   Without one ray of cheer.

Mamma taught me to say good things,
   Alike to low and high;
For little boys should always know
   "Kind words will never die."

I WILL BE THINE.

Oh! why have we thus strangely met!
   Is it stern fate's decree?
My heart is wildly beating yet—
   I find it throbs for thee.

Then let us sail our tiny bark
   Upon life's stormy sea,
And fan in flame the glimmering spark
   Of love thou hast for me.

I'll be thy life, thy love, thine all,
   In sunshine and in storm,
Till death's dread angel shall thee call
   To waft thy spirit home.

You ask of me my love, my soul;
   To thee it shall be given
O'er my short life to have control,
   Then anchor safe in heaven.

OUR STARS AND BARS.

UNFURL our glorious banner,
  In defiance let it fly;
We'll drive the foe from off our land,
  Or in the fray we'll die.
No matter on what bloody field—
  Near childhood home, or far—
Cover us with the bonnie blue flag
  That bears a single star.

Unfurl our glorious banner,
  The same our forefathers bore
When they fought the minions of King George,
  And drove them from our shore.
They gave them "Hail Columbia,"
  And Yankee Doodle-do,
As they raised aloft the stars and bars
  Of our bonnie banner blue.

Then unfurl our glorious banner,
  Let loose our dogs of war;
For upon the bloodiest field of strife,
  We'll follow our glittering star.
Ah! thickly studding the azure blue,
  As stars in the sky at even',
We look again—can it be true?
  Our flag has gained eleven.

Oh! unfurl our glorious banner,
  And proudly may it wave
From Maryland to the farthest point,
  Where sleeps a southern brave.
No matter on what bloody field—
  Near our loved home, or far—
Cover us with our bonnie blue flag,
  That has gained the eleventh star.

MOSES RECEIVING THE TEN COMMANDMENTS.

They stood by Mount Sinai,
  To view the tables of stone;
Which were handed down to Moses
  From God's lofty throne.

'Mid thunders most terrible,
  And dense clouds of smoke;
The Lord from his sacred Mount
  To Moses thus spoke:

"Restrain thee thy people,
  Let them come not too nigh;
For if they but see my face
  They surely must die.

"Take thou these two tables
  From out my sacred hand,
And tell thy people thus my word
  Forevermore shall stand."

MOONLIGHT.

The moon comes forth this evening,
  As in royal majesty,
And on the world her brightness
  Sheds alike for you and me.

Beneath the eastern horizon
  She first beams forth apace;
Then moving slowly onward
  She reaches the far west.

She casts her shadows on the ground,
  When crusted o'er with snow;
And shines so bright in harvest-time
  Alike on high and low.

A very queen she seems to be,
  With her great brilliant train;
Smiling on earth benignantly
  For all to praise her name.

THE YOUNG SOUTHERN HUNTERS.

    As with whistle and a bound,
    We clear each foot of ground,
And an eager pack of hounds on our track,
    With the hunter's merry horn
    We welcome the glad morn;
So there's naught that our jolly fellows lack.

    For the game we love so dear,
    In plenty we'll find here;
It needs but the healthy, vigorous chase
    To make it lose its cover,
    So at good aim topple over,
And we bag it with very good grace.

    Now we, with hunter's pride,
    Call our hounds to our side,
For our day's glorious sport is just done;
    Ah! they seem to know what's out,
    For they turn them straight about,
Making their quick tracks for home.

THE EXPLOSION OF THE *WESTFIELD*.

The sun was shining bright and clear
    Upon that Sabbath noonday;
Hundreds were loitering on the pier,
    Chasing dull care away;
When a vessel rode into the dock,
Quickly they all on board did flock.

Parents and children gathered there
    Simply for recreation,
Ne'er dreaming that gaunt death stood near
    To mount guard o'er the station;
And with his sickle to gather them in—
The man of the world, and the child without sin.

Great God! what means this terrible sound?
    Ah! 'tis the wail of despair.
Horrors! what sights are scattered around!
    Death reaps a harvest there;
And many who high in the air were flung
Found rest at last in their watery tomb.

But those who still on the vessel lay,
    Moaning and writhing in pain,
Strangers come, bear them gently away,
    In life ne'er to see them again:
For, ere the setting of another sun,
Their sufferings are over—to death they succumb.

CONSOLATION.

Through fairest fields above,
Safe in the Father's love,
    Roams your dear lost one;

Led by the Shepherd's hand,
To join the cherub band,
    As they go marching on.

Her infant prattle's o'er,
You'll hear it nevermore
    Within your earthly home.

Upwards your thoughts must fly,
Beyond the starry sky,
    Then say "Thy will be done."

EASTER MORN.

The words that ancient prophets spoke,
   In this great victory we'll win;
For Christ has risen; He hath broke
   All the bonds of death and sin.

Mary went at early dawn
   To the tomb to find her Lord.
The angel said: Why did ye come?
   See! he hath quit this dark abode.

There's the shroud his form was wrapt in,
   As he laid three days in the tomb.
He has bursted the fetters that bound him
   And has robbed the grave of its gloom.

Then shout the glad tidings this morning;
   For Christ, who laid three days dead,
Has risen at gray of the dawning,
   And death away captive has led.

GRATITUDE.

Full measure of gratitude, that's how it read
That letter—great stress on "Gratitude" laid.

With an air of sincerity, tho' I own it was selfish,
But I rather liked that, for you know I am elfish.

I was changed in a moment, as I read the Epistle—
Oh, my heart felt as light as the down of a thistle.

We met, and my heart gave a bound of delight;
I knew 'twas a clear case of love at first sight.

Now I thought that all feeling forever had fled,
And my love was buried away with the dead.

But not so it seems, for it flamed up so high,
Through sheer mortification, I was ready to cry.

Well! for long hours we held converse so sweet,
Till at length the lamps shed their light on the street.

Then he arose to take leave, when he called me
 "a treasure,"
"And of gratitude," said he, "I'll expect a full measure."

'Twas two years ago, I'll remember that day,
Though he that I write of is far, far away.

Well, we met once again: I was clasped to his heart;
He vowed as he held me, we never should part.

As our lips met then in one long, thrilling kiss,
And our hearts throbbed as one, with such rapturous bliss,

Then I know 'twas recorded by angels above,
Not *gratitude* only, but full measure of LOVE.

I have raised me an idol, to worship at will,
Through life's vicissitudes I'll cling to it still.

I'll always believe now in love at first sight,
Though ne'er was convinced till that very night,

When he kissed me and said, My little divinity,
Now I'm sure I have found at last my affinity.

SOUTHERN SPIRIT OF 1871.

Strike down to death all those who dare
Defy our rights we hold so dear,
   And desecrate our flag.

SHALL AMERICANS RULE AMERICA?

Americans, awake! awake!
And let this mighty nation shake
    With your firm resolution!
To keep intact your country's laws,
And mete out punishment to those
    Who stir up a commotion.

Strike! strike for freedom and your home,
And ye'll avert the awful doom
    That seems impending o'er thee;
See the base rabble, how they rush
Onward, Americans to crush,
    And in their fury spurn ye.

Put not to shame your noble sires,
Who, 'mid the Revolution fires,
    The yoke of thraldom broke!
Casting aside Britannia's band,
They made a free and happy land
    By each gallant, vigorous stroke

They swore them then in solemn mood,
By Warren's and by Sumpter's blood,
   'Mid war's desolation!
The tree of Liberty to plant,
And to posterity to grant
   Freedom's sweet consolation.

Then must the servile minions come
To overspread this land with gloom,
   And all our ties to sever?
Americans, arise! arise!
Let shouts of freedom rend the skies,
   And hills will echo, Never!

Ye men of might, awake! awake!
Put on thy strength, this nation shake
   From ocean shore to mountain crag;
Strike down to death all those who dare
Defy our rights we hold so dear,.
   And desecrate our flag.

THE DEATH OF THE YOUNG DRAGOON.

When bending in silence o'er his lone, narrow tomb,
Thinking so sorrowfully of his sad, early doom:
Oh, mourn not as one whose hopes have all fled,
Whose heart seems buried forever with the dead.

Let the young warrior rest, his troubles are o'er,
He'll arouse to the bugle-call on earth nevermore;
"On fame's eternal camping-ground his silent tent is spread,"
And history shall record his deeds with all the noble dead.

E'en Wide-Awake, his faithful friend on many
    a battle plain,
Shall never have to guard him more, or hear
    his voice again;
On many a field of battle he so nobly filled his
    part,
At last, when death's stern message came, he
    fell—shot through the heart.

But surely, if thou hast affliction's pathway trod,
Thou ne'er should doubt the goodness of your
    God;
Kindly He will His timely aid impart,
To cheer thy childless, lonely, drooping heart.

DEATH.

They call me cruel, 'tis not so,
   I am one sent from God;
Yet I cause the saddest tears to flow
   Upon the upturned sod.

In mercy I am often sent
   To ease poor mortal's pain,
And to urge the sinner to repent,
   Through me to live again.

There are bright fields beyond the skies
   Where I can never enter;
Still through me mortals must arise
   To reach their great Head-Centre.

I'm but a servant God doth send
   To call His children home;
His jewels He doth only lend,
   I gather them for His crown.

IS MY SISTER DEAD?

They call her dead, and is it so?
   And must my sister from me part?
Beloved was she by us below,
   So blest in spirit—pure in heart.

The bed of sickness racked her frame;
   With patience did she lie thereon;
Nor could she rise 'till death should claim
   That blessed spirit as its own.

The Master's voice called gently, "Come;
   The golden gates are open now,
Enter thy bright, celestial home,
   For with the angels thou shalt bow."

No doctor's aid, nor human skill,
   Can bring that spirit back again;
It rests in glory—and there still
   Forever with the Lord to reign.

What pain and suffering she endured
  No mortal tongue on earth can tell;
But she has reached that blessed abode,
  For Jesus has done all things well.

Weep not for her, ye friends, so dear,
  But wipe the tear from thy sad eye;
Go to her grave—she is not there,
  Then look, and say, that she's on high.

May we prepare to follow her,
  And live through life as she did live,
So when in judgment we'll appear
  A crown of glory we'll receive!

THE SILVER STREAM IN A SOLID ROCK.

Not many years ago, upon Evacuation morn,
   Two interesting little children left their play
To act a noble part, to lay the corner stone
   Of grandma's " brown stone mansion " of to-day,
Whose massive front looms up to view
   Before all who pass—" Fifth Avenue."

The girl, a tiny trowel took in hand,
   While the boy placed in a box some charms,
Papers, and coin of every stamp and land;
   Then they sealed it with masonic arms,
And buried it deep in the solid rock,
   To test old time's severest shock.

Ah! stern old rock, from out whose depth
   A fount of purest water sends,
Can'st thou not tell when thou wert cleft,
   And let us know what this portends?
Surely 'tis something bright for thee,
   Thou emblem of security.

Upon thine uncomplaining bosom stands,
   (Courting the admiration of the passer-by)
A gorgeous palace, built by human hands,
   Well worthy to be viewed with critic's eye,
Whilst thou art cast in nature's mould,
   And count thine age—by centuries told.

Yet an hundred years from now thou'lt stand
   A monument of grandeur of the past day,
Like a sentinel guarding his sleeping band;
   (While in truth) they're fallen into decay,
Thou'lt remain an hundred years from now,
   With thy sparkling waters yet sprinkling thy brow.

THE ASSASSINATION OF THE PRINCE OF ERIE.

Ye men of the Ninth! be great in your woe,
For the mighty has fallen, your chief is laid low;
Not upon the field of battle, nor in the bloody fray,
But th' hand of the assassin 'twas that stole his life away.

Oh, mourn for your chieftain, cut down in the pride
Of manhood's bright noonday, with none by his side
To warn him of danger that lurked in the hall,
Of the cowardly assassin by whose hand he should fall.

Now he sleeps his last sleep; your leader's work is done,
And ye've laid him to rest near his childhood's happy home,
Where the busy tongue of slander will ne'er reach him again,
And the generous-hearted guardsman shall never more complain. [*See remark.*]

O GOD! TAKE THOU HIS SOUL.

As death's dark waters near him roll,
   His wife, by anguish riven,
Cries, O my God! take Thou his soul,
   And anchor it in heaven.

Oh, what a volume in that prayer,
   Which fills the room of death;
To cause to flow the silent tear,
   And hold enchained the breath.

If Thou must take him, take his soul;
   Let angels waft it home;
Inscribe his name upon the scroll
   That hangs in heaven's high dome.

Take Thou his soul—wash out its stain,
   And make it pure and white;
Let it, O God, with Thee remain
   Forever in Thy sight.   [*See remark.*]

LOVE.

Ages ago the same tale was told:
   Love in a rose-bud lies hidden;
Life its bright pages of pleasure unfold,
   In a moment we read them unbidden;
So by night and by day, as time steals away,
   Oft mingling in life with the brilliant and gay,
Never dreaming that ought can dim its bright
   ray.

When the sun is obscure, and the sky is o'ercast,
High winds and rude waves engulf us at last,
Even then will our thoughts to our loved ones
   return,
Even then will the fire of love in us burn;
Love warms us to life, tho' struggling with fate;
Each ray brings us back from eternity's gate,
'Round and about us to cling evermore.

THE LAST WORDS OF A DYING YOUNG CHRISTIAN.

O, MOTHER, dear mother, come nigh me, I pray,
And remember the last words on earth I shall
    say,
Ere I approach the dark river of death,
Which will drown all my senses, and take
    away breath.

Listen! methinks I hear the angels' sweet song,
As they attune their bright harps all the day
    long.
Ah! they fly thro' space—they come nigh the
    shore;
See, mother, their bright forms—they beckon me
    o'er.

But whose yon grand form, so terribly bright?
Now, as He approaches, it dazzles my sight;

Yet his sweet voice assures me, its rich master-
 tone,
Like some grand swell of music, is luring me on.

My blood, ye believe, hath cleansed ye from sin,
To the courts of my Father I'll welcome ye in.
Oh, mother, farewell! my soul mounts—I fly;
'Tis sweet, oh, so sweet, in Jesus to die.

A VISION DURING ILLNESS.

In heaven above, where I behold
Harps with their numbers all untold,
Touched by seraphic fingers, play
Glory to God in endless day.

List! sweet music o'er me stealing
Takes away my sense, my feeling,
Lulls my pain, and sets me free
To catch a glimpse of heaven and thee.

Hark! loud music now begin,
Heaven with hallelujahs ring;
'Tis th' angelic choir which ne'er shall cease
In songs to praise their Prince of Peace.

But, oh, that bright and dazzling crown
Of Him who sits upon yon throne
Bursts now upon my vision fair,
That Christ, the judge of man, is near.

A VISION DURING ILLNESS.

Did that bright Being die for me?
Did'st hang upon the accursed tree?
The life-blood flowing from his side
He meekly bowed his head and died.

Ah, yes, He died, that we might live,
And unto Him our praises give,
So when in His Father's courts above
We'll join the angel-choir of love.

ON THE DEATH OF AN INFANT.

What little form is this
   That in this coffin lay?
'Tis an angel of perfect bliss,
   Whose spirit has soared away.

'Twas taken from its parents, young,
   Set free from earthly care;
Borne to rare fields beyond the tomb,
   To bud and blossom there.

To roam through paths of light
   With the great cherub-band,
Lisping sweet songs both day and night
   In that bright and happy land.

Oh, wish him not back again,
   In this great land of gloom;
Rather rejoice that he's free from pain,
   And lives beyond the tomb.

TO MY FOSTER-BROTHER.

In the silent night,
When the stars shone bright,
    And the breeze of summer swayed,
The trees to our right,
As they played in the light,
    Then would hide again in the shade.

Then the voice of mamma
Could be heard from afar,
    As she called, t'was time to go—
So would come the time
For closing the blind,
    Now I hear you exclaim—that's just so.

But now, alas!
Those times are all passed,
    Yet they live in my memory still;
I'll follow them back,
Through affection's track,
    And cherish them with a good will.

LIFE'S SILVER THREAD IS BROKEN.

Life's silver cord is broken,
   Earth's pilgrimage is o'er;
Her farewells gently spoken,
   She sleeps, to wake no more.

Tread lightly 'round the coffin
   That enshrines the early dead;
And bedew the floral offering
   With tears that ye do shed.

Ye'll not disturb her slumbers,
   For death his vigils keep;
No more she'll join thy numbers,
   But wherefore do ye weep?

God's jewels He but lendeth,
   He wants them for His crown;
His servant death he sendeth
   To bring those jewels home.

Your Lottie's death was peaceful—
  What need her friends ask more?
Her greetings will be blissful
  On Cannan's happy shore,

Where life's eternal morning
  Breaks o'er fair fields of light;
While she, with angels roaming,
  Is clothed in spotless white.

LINES ON THE DEATH OF MARY R——, OF WASHINGTON CITY.

FOLD the hands gently over her breast,
And take the last kiss ere you lay her to rest;
For her trials are over, her labors are done,
And the angels have whispered—"Sister, come home."

There's a home for her in the mansions above,
Where all is life, joy, peace and love;
They'll shout the glad tidings, loud praise shall be given,
When they welcome her thro' the bright portals of heaven.

Then shed not a tear when her grave you shall see,
She has broken sin's fetters, from sorrow set free!

Now the angels keep watch o'er her lone narrow bed
And whisper—"She sleepeth, your sister's not dead."

THE WRECK OF THE *PASINO*.

'Mid thunder's loud crash,
   In the wrathful sky,
And lightning's red gleam,
   As the sea, mountain high,
Rose in terrible grandeur
   In its awful unrest,
As 'twould fain shake some weight
   From its throbbing breast.

Then the brave captain cried:
   There's no hope of help now;
Let us die like true men,
   To our fate meekly bow,
Praying our sins
   May all be forgiven;
And our souls may be
   Reunited in heaven.

THE WRECK OF THE PISANO.

God of the sea! wilt Thou not hear
Thy children's frantic wail of despair?
No help is nigh—must we sink to sleep
In the cold embrace of the treacherous deep?

Yet another fierce shock,
　　Then 'mid appalling gloom,
That heroic band
　　Now awaited their doom:
So each manly heart
　　Has at last found rest;
And the sea seems cleared
　　Of the weight on its breast.

No marble monument
　　For them marks their graves;
They lie fathoms deep
　　'Neath the treacherous waves,
And the sea as though
　　For them she yet grieves;
A shroud of sea-weed
　　Continually weaves.

Now the aged mother,
　　And the loving young wife,
From their loved one has parted
　　Forever in life.

But remember, ye mourners,
    That hold me in dread,
That at the last day
    I must give up my dead.

So the shining waves
    Go rippling along;
As they seem to be singing
    This funeral song:
I cause the loved ones
    Of earth to part;
To rock them to sleep
    On my cold—cold heart.

Do ye wonder now,
    Why I tremble so,
As tho' to each wave
    I'm murmuring low?
Smooth out your ruffles
    And put by that frown,
We must hide the place
    Where the vessel went down.

AN ACROSTIC.

CONFIDENCE.

Gone from my gaze, but not forever
  E'en now stern duty calls thee hence,
Out upon thy business ever,
  Raise thee some rich recompense;
Go—my heart will still be true,
Ere now I sleep I'll pray for you.

When night her sable mantle draws,
And decks it o'er with glittering stars,
'Round thee my thoughts will ever twine
Regardless of the lapse of time;
E'en now I feel thy presence near,
Now trusting still, I'll not court fear.

THE SERENADE.

Pray, lady, awake and listen to me
While I sing of the love I bear unto thee.

Come, lady, awake, and throw me a kiss,
To fill up the measure of my earthly bliss.

From thy window, sweet one, a soft light is shed;
It leads me so nigh thee, it encircles my head.

O, list while I sing and attune my guitar,
For thou art my loved one, my bright guiding star.

My loved one, oh, hear me! I'm watching for you,
To throw just one kiss to thy lover so true.

Ah, I see thee at last, now, sweet one, good-night,
May thy slumbers be guarded by angels of light!

WALKING DOWN BROADWAY.

On a clear cold winter's morn,
    While walking down Broadway,
I met an handsome fellow,
    Who unto me did say:

'Tis very cold this morning;
    May I join you for a walk,
No one will think us strangers
    If you'll only with me talk?'

Although I do not know you,
    Yet I admire your carriage,
Who knows but this may yet result
    In a most happy marriage?

Your eyes are bright as stars,
    Your lips like cherries red,
It makes my heart go pit-a-pat,
    And whirls around my head.

THE SEA OF MATRIMONY.

WILL the captain of the *Prudence*
    Be faithful and true,
As the writer of this
    Will be faithful to you;
In calm and in storm
    With great breakers ahead,
Stand firm and manly,
    As though he had nought to dread?

Then make ready the yacht,
    Let her sails kiss the wind,
And I'll warrant we'll soon
    Leave all troubles behind,
For together we'll drink
    Of the cup of life's pleasure,
With our heart's true affection
    We'll fill up its measure.

TO A BACHELOR.

Art thou lonely?—so am I.
The chord of sympathy let us tie
    Round that heart thou say'st is broken.
If there's congeniality in our natures,
Pray, let us now be rational creatures.
    Accept from me this friendship's token.

FLIRTATION.

No, indeed! it will not be at any street corner,
Of that be assured, upon a lady's honor.
For I would not be a target
For every passer-by,
To throw me questioning glances,
Oh, no, not I——
But I'll step inside a store,
Which will not create alarm,
And will do my best to please you,
Which will not be any harm.

TAMMANY RING

THERE once was formed a mighty ring,
Considered strong and sound,
The centre-head was a stout old king,
With golden fetters bound.
All called him the "great-hearted,"
For while in gracious mood
With money he cheerfully parted,
To buy the poor fuel and food.

This director rose from nothing,
(A mender of old chairs);
But upon his family doting,
They put on mighty airs,
For he was worth great piles of gold,
And in bright gems did deal.
So, as he was just growing old,
On a grand scale began to steal.

Up rose some great reformers,
And sounded well this ring;
They found it was all hollow—
A worthless, rotten thing.
With force they struck upon it,
So asunder it straightway flew:
Under the fragments fell the whole clique,
With their great chieftain too.

"How are the mighty fallen!"
This fearless, thieving band,
The scorn of every honest man
That breathes throughout the land.
Let scorn meet them at every turn,
This "Great Boss" and his clan.
May the fires of indignation burn,
And place them under BAN!

THE GHOST OF PATTERLOO.

A SHADOWY form at the window,
   The right hand holding a light;
The left, raised—as if to hinder,
   From the curious, the ghastly sight.
For this form they behold without a head
Is that of a man just one month dead.

They said the house was haunted,
   So, in affright, the inmates fled
When a force of policemen, undaunted,
   Made search for the unknown dead,
When up in the garret, prostrate on the floor,
They found this form all covered with gore.

Firmly was grasped in his hand
    A candle—but minus a flame;
His head they found under a stand;
    In his pocket they found a name;
So they buried this hideous thing from view,
    And inscribed on his tombstone, "Poor Patterloo."

THE RIVAL SPIRITS.

The rival spirits of man you see,
Forever in his wake to be;
One is for good—the other ill,
You'll find them in his pathway still.

Oh man, to which the victory's due,
Is left entirely with you;
One tries the soul to bring to hell,
The other in bright realms to dwell.

Oft would I have fallen, had it not been
My good angel nigh me was always seen;
So all who hold the arch-fiend in dread
Lift high the cross—'Twill break his head.

Cross ye yourself when Satan is nigh,
When around you his poisonous darts do fly.
Call on your good angel, who'll guard you
    right well,
And guide you in safety forever to dwell.

ANGELS' SONG.

Rest in peace, thy toils are o'er,
   Sleep the sleep that knows no waking,
We'll guide thee safe on yonder shore,
   Where the glorious dawn of life is breaking.

Rest in peace; rest in peace;
   Thine earthly pilgrimage is o'er.
Rest in peace; rest in peace;
   We'll shout thy welcome to our shore.

VILLAGERS' BURIAL SONG.

Stranger, we lay thee down gently to sleep,
In the grave that we've made for thee, narrow
   and deep;

'Tis humble and lowly, but thou'lt rest there
  right well.
In peace we now leave thee—O, stranger,
  farewell!
Oh, stranger, farewell—
    Stranger, farewell!

FAIRY'S SONG.

Welcome, noble strangers!
  Welcome to our cave;
We're a band of rangers,
  We were born to save.
    In safety rest ye
      Here, we pray;
    Sleep, and we'll guard thee,
      Till the bright god of day
    Bid ye arise,
      And haste away.

CHILDREN'S BOAT SONG.

SINGING, singing merrily,
Childhood's hours are full of glee;
We are merry, gay, and bright,
Upon this lovely moonlight night.
Then merrily, merrily, let us sing,
While time is flitting on the wing,
For we're guided by sweet Luna's ray,
And we'll not go home till the break of day.

INCANTATION SONG.

May all the demons from below
Come forth and sit upon our foe.

Aye, all the fiends of hell beside,
Over his hated body stride.

With hideous dragons may he make his bed,
With moulten lava poured upon his head.

Come forth! come forth, come forth,
Ye demons from below the earth.

'Mid thunder, lightning, hail and rain,
Come dance upon the earth again.

Demons, come forth—astride—astride—
This body quick, or woe betide.

WITCHES' SONG.

THREE WITCHES.

Hail, sister! why hast thou called us thence?
Perchance to draw the nail from out the fence,
Or to punish for some great offence;
Ah, now it may be as we say,
The penalty of some offence to pay.

CHIEF WITCH.

Hark ye—hark ye, to me! this day,
Know'st thou a mortal dare to stray
Into our charmed circle?
'Tis he that I would have ye slay,
And it is for this
That I have summoned thee,
To do his life away—away—
That I now command ye.

ODE TO THE MOON.

Sweet Luna, I hail thee,
    Gentle queen of the night,
Shed thy sweet light on me,
    And guide me aright.
Oh, Luna, sweet Luna,
    Let thy silver light
Be encircled around me
    And guide me aright.

SONG IN THE DISTANCE.

Hail! all hail—
    Hail to our beautiful queen,
We bow before thee,
We all adore thee,
    And we live for our beautiful queen.

ESTRALDA'S SONG.

Oh, happy, happy, happy me!
　　This adoration pleases,
What! 'tis my noble band I see,
　　And hear them sing my praises.

Here's to thy health, my noble lord,
　　Faithful and trusty is thy sword;
While life shall last thou'lt be adored
　　By thine ever-faithful Estralda.

ANSWER.

BY APOLLYON.

'Tis here I swear, by Heaven,
　　This faithful love to prize,
Most precious boon to man is given,
　　To light his pathway to the skies.

THE KING'S PETITION.

O, Estralda, mine own,
Come wear ye my crown;
That at peace I may be
At peace I may be.

O, take thee my crown,
Estralda, mine own;
And forgive me, forgive me, I pray,
Or forever blot out this dark day.

ANSWER BY ESTRALDA.

Wear ye the crown
That thy treachery bought;
I forever disown
Thee, even in thought.

ANSWER BY ESTRALDA.

The contempt which I bear thee
 I will freely thee tell,
I command thee to leave me :
 Now, murderer—farewell !

CHORAL SONG.

We are happy, we are free,
Tempt us not, tempt us not;
True to our queen we'll ever be,
Till time our faithfulness shall blot.
Ever free—ever free,
Happy, happy, happy we.

Tempt us not with glittering baubles,
We have come through all our troubles;
Faithful to our queen—our own—
We all shall be while time rolls on.
Ever free—ever free,
Happy, happy, happy we.

We are happy, hear us say,
Conscience clear and hearts so light;
Ne'er by ambition led astray,
We keep the paths of truth in sight.
Gay and free—gay and free,
Happy, happy, happy we.

THE AUTHOR'S APPEAL AND ADIEU

WILL some fair daughter of dame fashion,
   Grant the author so much pleasure,
As to take in charge this little book,
   And peruse it at her leisure?

There's nought of envy, plot, or passion,
   Too gaudily clothed in any part;
Yet I send to you, with woman's trusting,
   The simple promptings of my heart.

Mighter pens great themes have dwelt on,
   With which your fancy soared away;
But I send to you my simple verses,
   Of things that transpire every day.

To soldier, sailor, sister and brother,
   My heart's best gift I send to you;
In this message of one hundred pages,
   And bid you all a kind adieu!

REMARKS AND EXPLANATIONS.

UNITED WE STAND.
The Reception of the Fifth Maryland Regiment by the Seventh Regiment, N. G. N. Y. The first Reunion since the late Civil War.

POOR PATTERLOO.
Upon occasion of a Poor Milkman being found murdered in an old house in Washington City.

MOSES RECEIVING THE TEN COMMANDMENTS.
This poem was written, when Nine Years Old, in Sunday School.

MOONLIGHT.
Was written when a child—while Jumping Rope.

SONGS.

From the Original Plays of Estralda and the Rival Spirits.

SHALL AMERICANS RULE AMERICA.

Written on the occasion of the Orange Riot in New York City, July 12th, 1871, showing the Southern spirit of 1871—ten years after the War. Counter-piece to Our Stars and Bars— "We know no North, no South, no East, no West, but keep step to the Music of the Union."

TO THE GALLANT NINTH REGIMENT.

During the Orange Riot, on the 12th day of July, as the Mob had nearly reached the Grand Opera House, in which sat the late Col. Fisk attending to business. He rushed out, in plain clothes, and joined his regiment, but was soon wounded in the foot. When he heard of the death of the Three Guardsmen, he said: "Buy them a plot in Woodlawn, and spare no expense for their funeral."

KIND WORDS WILL NEVER DIE.
Written upon the occasion of a little Southern boy visiting the camp of Union Soldiers, during the late Rebellion.

EXPLOSION OF THE WESTFIELD.
The Westfield was an Excursion Boat running from New York to Staten Island. The terrible disaster occurred on a beautiful Sunday morning, in the Summer of 1871.

THE BRAVE BOYS IN BLUE.
Dedicated to the Policemen of New York City, on occasion of the Orange Riot, July 12th, 1871.

O GOD! TAKE THOU HIS SOUL.
While Col. Fisk was dying, his wife uttered this prayer while kneeling at his bedside.

'TWAS BUT A DREAM.
(I dreamed this dream, and wrote it down) just three nights before the assassination of Col. J. Fisk.

BOYS, THAT FLAG MUST FALL.

The last words of Col. Ellsworth, at Alexandria, Va.

ALEXIS CELEBRATING THE BIRTHDAY OF HIS SISTER-IN-LAW.

This happened upon our National Thanksgiving Day.

THE TWO ALEXANDERS.

Emperor Alexander the Second liberating the Serfs.

THE TWO GREAT OAKS.

"The Great Oak," The magnanimous Col. Fisk.—"The Lesser Oak," Stokes, his murderer.—"The Clinging Vine," his Wife,—and "The Bold Plotter," is the Mansfield, the Whited Sepulchre.

OUR STARS AND BARS.

The Southern Spirit of 1861.

DEATH OF THE YOUNG DRAGOON.

Words of Comfort to a Mother. Charles Canfield, of the Second U. S. Cavalry, killed at Beverly Ford, Va., 1863.

DEATH OF THE CHRISTIAN HERO.

Gen. Robert E. Lee was Commander of the Confederate forces during the Rebellion. (It is said that he died of a broken heart.) His residence was "Arlington, the magnificent estate opposite Washington City, which was the residence of the late Geo. Washington Park Custis, Step-Grandson of Gen. Geo. Washington."

THE WRECK OF THE PASINO.

Captain Alexander Roberts went down with all on board this vessel, in the Gulf of Mexico, Sept. 21st, 1867.

www.ingramcontent.com/pod-product-compliance
Lightning Source LLC
Chambersburg PA
CBHW020056170426
43199CB00009B/305